Knock! Knock!

Who Was There?

by Brian Elling

illustrated by Nancy Harrison and Andrew Thomson

Penguin Workshop

For Paula—BE

To Rhia—AT

PENGUIN WORKSHOP
An Imprint of Penguin Random House LLC, New York

Copyright © 2018 by Penguin Random House LLC. All rights reserved.
Published by Penguin Workshop, an imprint of Penguin Random House LLC, New York.
PENGUIN and PENGUIN WORKSHOP are trademarks of Penguin Books Ltd.
WHO HQ & Design is a registered trademark of Penguin Random House LLC.
Printed in the USA.

Visit us online at www.penguinrandomhouse.com.

Library of Congress Control Number: 2018933533

ISBN 9780515159325   10 9 8 7

CONTENTS

Milton Hershey

SAPPY CELEBRITIES

What does Elvis Presley do in a fire?
Rock, drop, and roll!

What did Walt Disney say when he went to the doctor?
"*Dis-knee* hurts!"

Knock! Knock!
Who's there?
Hershey.
Hershey who?
Her-shey-t of paper says, "Milton loves chocolate!"

How does Dolly Parton
like to count?
From one to *Ten-nessee*!

**Knock!
Knock!**
Who's there?
Dishes.
Dishes who?
Dish-es **a meal cooked
by** Julia Child!

Why was <u>Aretha Franklin</u>
so nice to old people?
Because she had so many
Grammys!

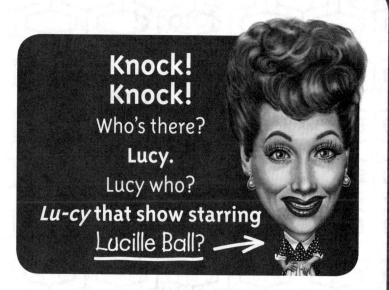

Knock! Knock!
Who's there?
Lucy.
Lucy who?
Lu-cy that show starring Lucille Ball? →

Why did Annie Oakley
get accused of stealing?
Because she was always *taking aim*!

Knock! Knock!

Who's there?

A wreath.

A wreath who?

A-wreath-a **Franklin is the Queen of Soul!**

Knock! Knock!

Who's there?

Norma Lee.

Norma Lee who?

Norma-Lee, **I don't like scary movies. But** Alfred Hitchcock's **are amazing!**

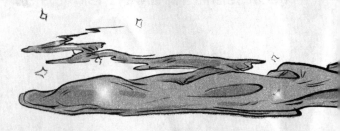

What did Harry Houdini
say on Halloween?

"Trick or *trick*!"

Why was Elton John so tired
after the concert?

Because his costume
weighed an *El-ton*!

Who is Santa's favorite
rock-and-roll singer?
Elves Presley!

**Knock!
Knock!**
Who's there?
Andy Warhol.
Andy Warhol who?
Andy *War-hol*
kinds of wigs!

Why did Milton Hershey's
wife marry him?
She wanted lots of Hershey's *kisses*.

Knock!
Knock!

Who's there?

Reggae.

Reggae who?

***Reggae* or not, we're going to
listen to a <u>Bob Marley</u> song!**

Knock! Knock!
Who's there?
Police.
Police who?
Police don't turn off that <u>Beatles</u> music!

Knock! Knock!
Who's there?
Mice.
Mice who?
Mice-cream delivery for <u>Walt Disney</u>!

Knock! Knock!
Who's there?
Sir.
Sir who?
Sir-iously, Elton John is such a talented musician!

Why does <u>Bob Dylan</u> vacation in Las Vegas?

He likes *Dylan* cards!

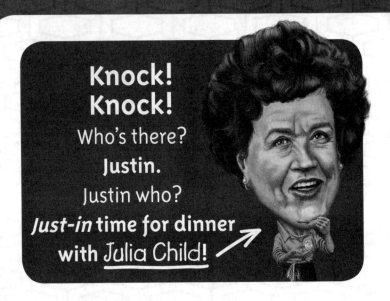

Knock! Knock!
Who's there?
Justin.
Justin who?
Just-in time for dinner with <u>Julia Child</u>! →

Knock! Knock!
Who's there?
Amal.
Amal who?
Am-al **shook up over** Elvis Presley!

Why was Aretha Franklin so good at snapping her fingers? Because of her *rhy-thumbs*!

Knock! Knock!
Who's there?
Radio.
Radio who?
Radi-o not, here comes another Elvis song!

Which famous jazz musician
was also a weight lifter?

Louis *Armstrong!*

Where did Milton Hershey go when he wanted a glass of milk? To a *chocolate bar.*

Why did everyone scream when Lucille Ball went to the aquarium? Because there was a *Loose-eel* in there!

Knock! Knock!
Who's there?
Marshall.
Marshall who?
***Martial* arts made** Bruce Lee **famous!**

PUNCH-LINE PATRIOTS AND PRESIDENTS

How does President Obama dance?
Ba-rack-ing back and forth!

**Knock!
Knock!**
Who's there?
I Otto.
I Otto who?
**I *Ot-to* know that
Washington was
the first president!**

14

Why were Betsy Ross's feet tired?

Because of her American Indepen-*dance*!

Knock! Knock!
Who's there?
Wendy.
Wendy who?
Wen-dy king needs protection, call Joan of Arc!

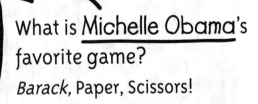

What is Michelle Obama's favorite game?

Barack, Paper, Scissors!

Where did George Washington go before he went to Valley Forge? Valley *Threege*.

Knock! Knock!
Who's there?
Musket.
Musket who?
Mus-ket to the
Alamo to meet
Davy Crockett!

What was President Lincoln's favorite sandwich?
Abraham and cheese!

Why did Davy Crockett wear a crown?
Because he was *King* of the Wild Frontier!

Knock! Knock!
Who's there?
Avenue.
Avenue who?
Aven-ue heard of Paul Revere?

Why did <u>Joan of Arc</u> fight in the Hundred Years' War?

Because she didn't want it to become the Hundred *and One* Years' War.

What was Alexander Hamilton's favorite sandwich?

Hamilton and cheese!

Why did Betsy Ross wear long dresses?

To cover her *colo-knees*!

Why did Paul Revere ride a horse when the British were attacking?

To warn his . . . *Neiggghhh-bors!!!*

Why did Hillary Clinton win the marathon?

Because she was the *first lady* to cross the finish line!

Knock! Knock!
Who's there?
War.
War who?
War there any presidents better than Abraham Lincoln?

Knock! Knock!
Who's there?
Michelle.
Michelle who?
Mi-chelle phone is ringing
and it's Mrs. Obama!

Knock! Knock!
Who's there?
Aaron.
Aaron who?
Aa-ron into
<u>Alexander Hamilton</u>
the other day!

What is President Obama's favorite food?
Barack of lamb!

What floor of the White House has the best coffee?
The *ground* floor!

What does Supreme Court Justice <u>Sonia Sotomayor</u> like in her drink?
Just-*ice*!

Why did <u>Mrs. Clinton</u> make the president laugh?
Because her jokes were *hillary*-ous!

Knock! Knock!
Who's there?
Jen.
Jen who?
Jen-**eral** Washington!

Which president liked lasers?
<u>Ronald *Ray-gun*</u>!

Knock! Knock!

Who's there?

Kennedy

Kennedy who?

Kenn-Eddy come play on the White House lawn?

Knock! Knock!

Who's there?

I'm Obama.

I'm Obama who?

I'm *O-ba-ma-self* out here!

Knock! Knock!
Who's there?
Theodore.
Theodore who?
Theo-dore is open,
President Roosevelt!

What did Sonia Sotomayor say when she took off her shoes?
"Odor! Odor in the court!"

What did the sheep say when he saw President Obama?
"Hi, *Baaaaa-rack*!"

What did George Washington do when his teeth fell out?

He got *presi*-dentures!

What is Michelle Obama's favorite tongue twister?

"She sells *Michelles* by the seashore."

What is <u>Clara Barton</u>'s favorite type of fish?

A *nurse* shark!

When did Abraham Lincoln make meatballs?

During the *Spaghettisburg Address.*

Which US president had antlers?
Theodore *Moosevelt*!

**Knock!
Knock!**
Who's there?
So.
So who?
So-**ing was Betsy Ross's
favorite thing to do!**

What does
<u>Ben Franklin</u>
say on
Halloween?
"*Elec-trick*
or treat!"

What happened to Joan of Arc after she went to war?

Her popularity *sword*!

Why does Sonia Sotomayor like tennis so much?

Because she loves going to *court*!

What did Johnny Appleseed say when his tree sprouted?

"*Seedling* is believing!"

SUPER SILLY SCIENTISTS

Knock! Knock!
Who's there?
Yukon.
Yukon who?
Yu-kon **always count on**
George Washington Carver!

Why did Galileo see the glass as half full?
Because he's a *fill*-osopher!

Why did <u>Ben Franklin</u> put down his experiment?

Because he was interested in *lightening*.

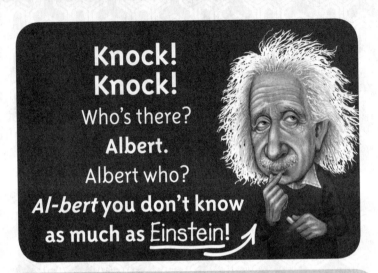

Knock! Knock!
Who's there?
Albert.
Albert who?
Al-bert you don't know as much as <u>Einstein</u>!

Why did **Marie Curie** listen to music?
She loved *radio-activity*!

Knock! Knock!
Who's there?
Manny.
Manny who?
Manny chimpanzees are friends with **Jane Goodall**!

Knock! Knock!
Who's there?
Water.
Water who?
Wat-er you waiting for? Let's go diving with Jacques Cousteau!

What did the king say when he learned about gravity?
"Out with the old and in with the *Newton!*"

Knock! Knock!
Who's there?
Sabina.
Sabina who?
Sa-bin-a long time since we saw Marie Curie!

Knock! Knock!
Who's there?
Einstein.
Einstein who?
Ein-stein home tonight to study physics!

What did Sir Isaac Newton tell his Little League team?
Keep your *Isaacs* on the ball!

Why did Charles Darwin like horse races?
Because he loved to watch them *Galap-agos!*

What did <u>Steve Irwin</u> drink
when it was cold outside?

Hot *croc-olate!*

Knock! Knock!
Who's there?
Darwin.
Darwin who?
*Dar-win-***dow is wide open!**

Why did Albert Einstein live close to his family?
So he could prove his theory of *relatives-ity*!

Knock! Knock!
Who's there?
Maya.
Maya who?
*"May-***animals are my best friends," said** <u>Jane Goodall</u>!

Knock! Knock!
Who's there?
Iguana.
Iguana who?
I-guana **watch** <u>Steve Irwin</u> **on TV!**

Why didn't Galileo want a surprise birthday party?
He wanted to *planet* himself!

What did Charles Darwin say when he lost the chess game?
"*Darwinning* isn't everything!"

Knock! Knock!
Who's there?
Newton.
Newton who?
New-tons of scientists, but none as famous as <u>Sir Isaac</u>!

What did Galileo's cat say when he first saw the moons of Jupiter?
"Astrono-meow!"

What's the first thing Charles Darwin learned at school?
His A, B, *speCies*!

Knock! Knock!
Who's there?
Panther.
Panther who?
Panth-er no pants, Steve Irwin sure loved animals!

Why didn't people believe <u>George Washington Carver?</u>

Because they thought he was *pea*-nuts!

AMUSING AUTHORS

Knock! Knock!
Who's there?
Hobbit.
Hobbit who?
Ho-bbit we go to the library and read a J. R. R. Tolkien book?

Why did Mark Twain turn in his book report late?
Because it wasn't *Huckleberry Finn*-ished!

Knock!
Knock!
Who's there?
Beecher.
Beecher who?
Bee-cher you can't stop reading
that Harriet Stowe **book,**
***Uncle Tom's Cabin**!*

What game did <u>Beatrix Potter</u>
play while she was writing
The Tale of Peter Rabbit?
Hopscotch!

Knock! Knock!
Who's there?
Sawyer.
Sawyer who?
Saw-yer **reading a book by** Mark Twain!

How did Laura Ingalls Wilder hear about becoming a writer? She listened with her pion-*ears*!

Why did Mark Twain run out of the ocean?
He saw a *Huckleberry Finn* swimming right at him!

Knock! Knock!
Who's there?
Oliver.
Oliver who?
O-liv-er, but not as much as I love reading a Charles Dickens **book!**

Why did Maurice Sendak go to the zoo?
Because that's *Where the Wild Things Are*!

Knock! Knock!
Who's there?
Kinney.
<u>Kinney</u> who?
Kinn-ey really write
so many books
about a wimpy kid?

What did Laura Ingalls's mom
say when she was up too late?
"It's *pasture* bedtime!"

Which playwright is also a great cook?
Will-yum Shakespeare!

Knock! Knock!

Who's there?

Canoe.

Canoe who?

Can-oe **tell me what books** Laura Ingalls Wilder **wrote?**

What did Jacob Grimm say to his brother, Wilhelm, when he got a cold?

"*Grimm* and bear it!"

Knock! Knock!

Who's there?

Maya.

Maya who?

Maya **have** Ms. Angelou's **book of poems?**

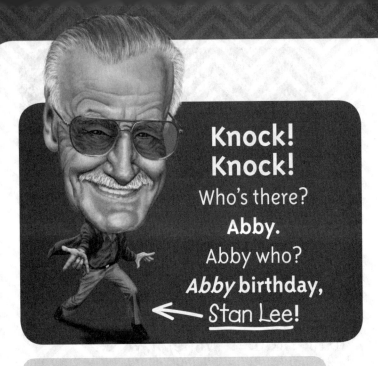

Knock! Knock!
Who's there?
Abby.
Abby who?
Abby birthday,
← Stan Lee!

Why did Maya Angelou go
outside during the blizzard?
To make snow *Angelous*!

Why did Charles Dickens
use crutches?
Because he *Oliver Twisted* his ankle!

Knock! Knock!
Who's there?
Tolkien.
Tolkien who?
Tolkien about famous authors is so fun!

During what month does Stan Lee like to write about Spider-Man?
In *Web*-ruary!

Knock! Knock!
Who's there?
Allan.
Allan who?
A-llan my pen to Edgar Allan Poe, but he never gave it back.

Why did the <u>Brothers Grimm</u> always have a messy room? Because of all their *litter*-ature!

Knock! Knock!
Who's there?
Twain.
Twain who?
Twain your dog to write a best-selling book!

Why did **Mr. Verne** give his wife a diamond ring?
Because she loved *Jules*!

What do playwrights like to drink?
*Milk-**Shakespeare**s!*

Knock! Knock!
Who's there?
Wand.
Wand who?
Wand-er around the library and you'll find a J. K. Rowling **book!**

What did Beatrix Potter forget to bring to the barbecue?

Hamburger *bun*-nies!

Which holiday song did <u>Laura Ingalls Wilder</u> like to sing?

"*Ingalls* bells! *Ingalls* bells! *Ingalls* all the waaaay!"

Knock! Knock!
Who's there?
Candice.
Candice who?
Can-dice **play by**
William Shakespeare
get any better?

Why did J. K. Rowling get an A in English class?
Because she knew how to *spells*.

Where does **Harriet Stowe** like to watch football games?
In the *Beecher-s!*

51

Knock! Knock!
Who's there?
Maurice Sendak.
Maurice Sendak who?
Maurice, *Sendak* book of yours to the publisher!

What's the title of J. R. R. Tolkien's book series about hobbits who play ice hockey?
The Lord of the *Rinks*!

What do you call <u>Charles Dickens</u> when he's scared of the dark?
Charles *Chickens*!

Knock! Knock!

Who's there?

Eddie.

Eddie who?

Eddie-body read any good Edgar Allan Poe **stories?**

What did Beatrix Potter do after she got married?

She went away on her *bunny* moon!

How can you tell if the <u>Brothers Grimm</u> are happy?

They wag their *fairy tales*!

Knock! Knock!

Who's there?

Harriet.

Harriet who?

Harriet up! Ms. Beecher Stowe **is at the door!**

Why couldn't the hobbit play any arcade games?

He left his *Tolkien-s* at home!

Why did <u>Roald</u> buy lots of tiny dresses?

For his *Dahl*!

54

Why was <u>Laura Ingalls Wilder's</u> house so little?

Because she lived in *Minne*-sota!

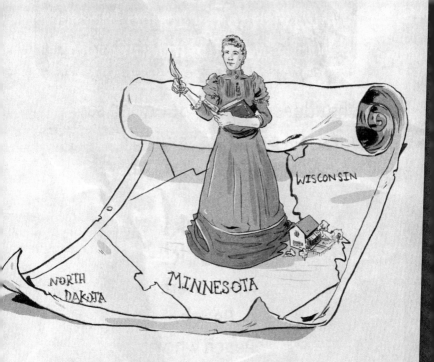

Knock! Knock!

Who's there?

Iowa.

Iowa who?

Iowa **visit to the** Laura Ingalls **Wilder Museum in Minnesota!**

What does Harriet Beecher say when she practices singing?

"Do! Re! Mi! Fa! *Stowe*! La! Ti! Do!"

Knock! Knock!

Who's there?

Peach.

Peach who?

Peach **book by** Roald Dahl **is more amazing than the last!**

Why did the author of *Alice in Wonderland* go to his neighbor's house on Christmas?
To do some <u>Lewis Carroll</u>ing!

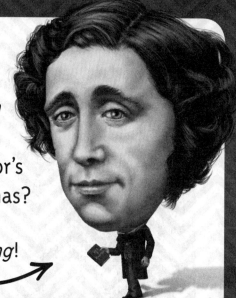

Why did *J. R. R. Tolkien* quit writing?
He thought it was a bad *hobbit*.

Knock! Knock!
Who's there?
Hamlet.
Hamlet who?
Ham-let me in, so I can meet Shakespeare!

**Knock!
Knock!**
Who's there?
Harry.
Harry who?
Harry up!
J. K. Rowling
**is signing
autographs!**

Why did Mr. Sendak go to the candy store?

He wanted *Maurice's* peanut butter cups!

Where did Edgar Allan Poe get his badge?

From the *poe*-lice academy!

Knock! Knock!
Who's there?
Will.
Will who?
Will Shakespeare **come out and play?**

Why did Laura Ingalls Wilder go to church a lot?
Because her house was on the *prayer*-ie!

How come <u>Beatrix Potter</u> never made a left turn?
Because she was a *writer*!

Why do J. K. Rowling's plants always look so pretty?

Because she knows a good *Potter*.

WACKY WORLD LEADERS

Why did <u>Princess Diana</u> like the ocean?

Because she was the Princess of *Wales*!

Knock! Knock!
Who's there?
Roy.
Roy who?
Roy-al family members, like <u>Queen Victoria</u>, shouldn't have to knock!

Knock! Knock!
Who's there?
Dewey.
Dewey who?
De-wey **know anyone smarter than** Winston Churchill?

Why did Queen Victoria always measure things? Because she was a *ruler*!

Why do Tibetan monks like to go to the zoo? To see the Dalai *Lama*!

Why couldn't the British army find Mahatma?
Because he was already _Gan-dhi_!

Knock! Knock!
Who's there?
Cesar.
Cesar who?
Ces-ar the signs I made for the protest with Mr. Chavez!

Which civil rights leader loved the library?
Book-er T. Washington!

Why did Cesar Chavez like bowling so much?
Because of all the *strikes*!

Why is it always so wet in England?
Because of **Queen Victoria**'s *reign*!

Knock! Knock!
Who's there?
Roman!
Roman who?
Roman around with Julius Caesar is exciting!

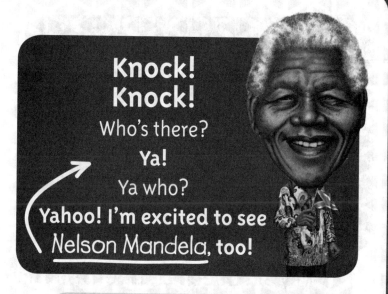

Knock! Knock!
Who's there?
Ya!
Ya who?
Yahoo! I'm excited to see Nelson Mandela, **too!**

How did King Tut say hello to a pyramid?
"*Hi*-roglyphics!"

Why did Princess Diana get arrested?
The detective found her finger-*prince*!

Knock! Knock!
Who's there?
Ides.
Ides who?
Ides **rather not be around** Caesar **during the month of March!**

Why did Queen Elizabeth scream when she looked in the mirror?

Because she accidentally put on the crown *ghouls*!

Why did King Tut go to bed?

Because his *mummy* told him to!

Why didn't Queen Victoria drink coffee?
Because she's royal-*tea*!

Knock! Knock!
Who's there?
Doughnut.
Doughnut who?
Dough-nut talk to Queen Elizabeth → without bowing!

Why did Alexander the Great become famous after taking over Persia?
Because he would *Babyl-on* about it all day!

Why did King Tut go to the dentist?
E-gypt his tooth!

What did Francis say to the people outside the Vatican? "Never give up *pope*!"

Why did Queen Elizabeth sweep the floor? Because she liked things nice and *queen*!

Knock! Knock!
Who's there?
Icon.
Icon who?
***I-con* think of a lot of people who were helped by** Cesar Chavez!

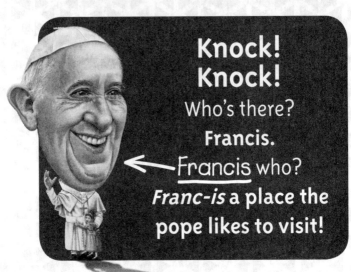

Knock! Knock!
Who's there?
Francis.
← <u>Francis</u> who?
Franc-is a place the pope likes to visit!

When did Cesar Chavez like to protest?
In *March*!

What did
<u>Winston Churchill</u>
say after he won
World War II?

"You *Winston*,
you lose some!"

Knock! Knock!
Who's there?
Defeat.
Defeat who?
De-feet of
Alexander the Great
really hurt after walking to India!

Knock! Knock!
Who's there?
Nobel.
Nobel who?
**No-bel on the door.
So Nelson Mandela had to knock!**

Knock! Knock!
Who's there?
Washington.
Washington who?
Washing-TONS of Booker T. Washington's laundry!

Knock! Knock!
Who's there?
India.
India who?
In-dia house next door lives Mahatma Gandhi!

What did Cesar Chavez say to the left-handed farm workers?
"I'll fight for your *rights*, too!"

SIDESPLITTING SPORTS STARS

Why did Babe Ruth spill so much water?

Because he used to be a *pitcher*.

Knock! Knock!
Who's there?
It's Jerrold.
It's Jerrold who?
It's Jerr-old friend, Muhammad Ali! ➡️

Why doesn't anyone want to eat lunch with <u>Serena and Venus Williams</u>?

Because they only *serve* tennis balls!

Knock! Knock!

Who's there?

Handsome.

Handsome who?

Handsome of Roberto Clemente's **awards to me!**

How do Venus and Serena Williams start a game of hide-and-seek?

They count from one to *ten-nis*!

Why did <u>Derek</u> play by the rules?

So that people wouldn't think he was a <u>*Jeter*</u>!

75

What's the most important ingredient in <u>Jackie Robinson</u>'s pancake recipe?

A good *batter*!

Why are Venus and Serena Williams always using their computers?
Because they love the *net*!

Knock! Knock!
Who's there?
Ketchup.
Ketchup who?
I can't *ketch-up* to Jesse Owens!

**Knock!
Knock!**
Who's there?
Sarah.
Sarah who?
Sar-ah **doctor in the house?**
Muhammad Ali
just got knocked out!

What happened when
Jesse Owens hurt his ankle?
He started *O-lymping*!

What was
Roberto Clemente's
favorite soup?
Clam-ente chowder!

How did Roberto Clemente get into the Baseball Hall of Fame? By being in the *right field* at the right time!

Knock! Knock!
Who's there?
Nadya.
Nadya who?
Nad-ya head if you like Venus and Serena Williams!

What does
Wayne <u>Gretzky</u>

like to eat when he's
not playing hockey?
Iceberg-ers!

How did Jackie Robinson
stay cool in the summer?
By sitting near his *fans*.

Why was Muhammad Ali so funny?
His jokes always had great *punch* lines!

**Knock!
Knock!**
Who's there?
Ollie.
Ollie who?
Muhammad **Ollie, the famous boxer!**

Knock! Knock!
Who's there?
Jesse.
Jesse who?
Je-sse how fast Jesse Owens can run?

What kind of dishes does Jackie Robinson have in his kitchen?
Home *plates*!

What did Derek Jeter say when his baseball mitt was stuck?
"Just give it a *Yank-ees*!"

What was Muhammad Ali's favorite drink?
Fruit *punch*!

Knock! Knock!
Who's there?
Olive.
Olive who?
O-live **to watch** Venus and Serena Williams **play tennis!**

Why did <u>Babe Ruth</u> get blamed when his neighbor's house disappeared?

Because they knew he could make a *home run*!

EXUBERANT EXPLORERS

Knock! Knock!
Who's there?
Mandy.
Mandy who?
Man-dy lifeboats!
Christopher Columbus
is heading to America!

How do pirates like their ships?
Plank and simple!

What is <u>Neil Armstrong</u>'s favorite state to visit?

NASA-chusetts!

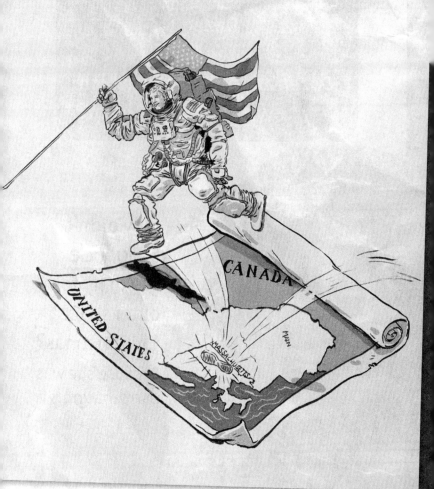

**Knock!
Knock!**
Who's there?
Dozen.
Dozen who?
Dozen anybody know which
way Lewis and Clark went?

Why didn't
Sally Ride
get to fly to
outer space
for Christmas?

Because she was
astro-naughty!

What did <u>Jacques Cousteau</u> say when he saw an orca for the first time?

"Whale, whale, whale, what do we have here?"

What type of music did Neil Armstrong like?

Rocket and roll!

Knock! Knock!
Who's there?
Wanda.
Wanda who?
Wanda around the skies with Amelia Earhart!

Knock! Knock!

Who's there?

Army.

Army who?

**"*Ar-my* pirates ready to set sail?"
asked <u>Blackbeard</u>!**

Knock! Knock!
Who's there?
Ice.
Ice who?

Ice see you've met **Ernest Shackleton, the great polar explorer!**

How did Neil Armstrong tie his shoes?
With an astro-*knot*!

Why was Amelia Earhart such a great pilot?
She had a really positive *altitude*!

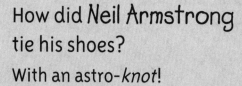

Knock! Knock!
Who's there?
Aardvark.
Aardvark who?
Aard-vark **all the way to Australia to see** <u>Steve Irwin</u>**'s zoo!**

What did people say when Amelia Earhart's plane mysteriously disappeared?
"The *pilot* thickens!"

What did Sir Shackleton say when he first saw penguins in Antarctica?
"Look at those *brrrrrrrr*ds!"

What did Magellan's father say when he set out to sea? "Son, you're a *ship* off the old block!"

What did <u>Genghis Khan's</u> cat like to call him? *Em-purrer*!

Knock! Knock!
Who's there?
Lou.
Lou who?
Lou-nar Control to Neil Armstrong, you are cleared for your moonwalk!

What did Ferdinand do when he woke up with bed head? He put some *Ma-gell-an* his hair!

Knock! Knock!
Who's there?
Cousteau.
Cousteau who?
Cousteau your scuba gear on Jacques's ship!

Why did Steve Irwin hire a crocodile to captain his boat?
He needed a good navi-*gator*!

Why do cows like Neil Armstrong?
Because he was the first man on the *mooooooooon*!

Why did Christopher sail ships across the Atlantic?

Because he was tired of taking the Colum-*bus*!

Knock! Knock!
Who's there?
Snow.
Snow who?
Snow way Ernest Shackleton would miss a trip to Antarctica!

How can you tell when <u>Daniel Boone</u> is sad?

He gets a fron-*tear* in his eye!

Knock! Knock!
Who's there?
Boat.
Boat who?
Boat the Atlantic and Pacific Oceans were sailed by Magellan!

Where did Ernest Shackleton keep his money when he went to Antarctica?
In a *snowbank*!

Who helped Steve Irwin give out Christmas presents to baby crocodiles?
Santa *Jaws*!

Knock! Knock!
Who's there?
Dwayne.
Dwayne who?
Dwayne the pool or we'll never stop playing Marco Polo!

Who is Sir Ernest Shackleton's favorite relative?
Aunt Arctica!

Why was Neil Armstrong so hungry?
He forgot to eat his *launch*!

Knock! Knock!
Who's there?
Lawn.
Lawn who?
Lawn-ch for Neil Armstrong in five, four, three, two, one!

Why did Amelia Earhart attempt to fly around the world?
Because life at home was too *plane*!

Where did their female guide put Lewis's and Clark's travel journals?
In her *Sack*-agawea!

95

Why was it so hard to catch **Blackbeard**?
Because his escape route was so *scurvy*!

What did **Daniel Boone** write in his holiday card?
"Peace on Earth and good *wilderness* to all!"

What did <u>Amelia Earhart</u> wear when she had to fly in a storm?
Her long *thunder*wear!

IRONIC INVENTORS

How did the inventor of
the Model T count his cars?
One, two, three, Ford!

**Knock!
Knock!**
Who's there?
Digital.
Digital who?
Dig-i-tal all your
friends that
Bill Gates
is coming over?

Why did the <u>Wright Brothers'</u> cat like airplanes so much?
Because of the *purr-peller*!

Knock!
Knock!
Who's there?
CD.
CD who?
C-D computer
<u>Steve Jobs</u> **designed?**

What did Henry Ford say when he opened his first car factory?

"I'm *wheelie* excited!"

Why did Thomas Edison read so much about electricity?

He liked *current* events.

Why did Steve Jobs
cut down a tree?
Because he needed to *log*
on to his computer!

What did Henry Ford say when
his car wouldn't start?
"I *au-to* do something about that!"

**Knock!
Knock!**
Who's there?
Bright.
Bright who?
Bright or wrong, <u>Edison</u>
invented the lightbulb!

Knock!
Knock!
Who's there?
The cargo.
The cargo who?
The car-go **faster if it's**
one of <u>Henry Ford</u>'s!

Why did Alexander Graham Bell
wear so much jewelry?
Because he loved *rings*!

Why was Steve Jobs late to the office?
He had *a hard drive*!

Knock! Knock!

Who's there?

Alex.

Alex who?

Alex-plain how a telephone works, but <u>Alexander Graham Bell</u> is better at it!

Why did Steve Jobs's computer squeak?

Because he stepped on the mouse!

Knock! Knock!
Who's there?
Backup disc.
Backup disc who?
Backup disc car! We forgot to pick up Bill Gates!

Why did Thomas Edison invent the lightbulb?

Because the *heavy* bulb was too hard to carry!

Knock!
Knock!

Who's there?

Isabel.

Isabel who?

Is-a-bel ringing? Or is that <u>Alexander Graham Bell</u> calling on his new telephone?

Why does Bill Gates eat so fast?
Because of his *megabytes*!

Knock!
Knock!
Who's there?
Annie.
Annie who?
Annie-**body see** Henry Ford
driving his new car?

Why did <u>Orville</u>
<u>and Wilbur</u>
<u>Wright</u> like
to stay inside?
Because they were
in-ventors!

Why did the inventor of the telephone like s'mores so much? Because of the Alexander Graham *crackers*!

Knock! Knock!
Who's there?
Iona.
Iona who?
Iona **computer that was developed by** Steve Jobs.

Where did Walt Disney sleep when he went camping?
On an *Ep-cot*!

ECCENTRIC ARTISTS AND ENTERTAINERS

**Knock!
Knock!**
Who's there?
Vinci.
Vinci who?
Vin-ci comes home, tell her
Leonardo is here!

What did <u>Jim Henson</u> do when the floor was dirty?
He tried to *Mopp-it*!

Knock! Knock!
Who's there?
Cher.
Cher who?
Cher **would be nice to play a** Milton Bradley **game!**

What's outside the castle where Wolfgang Amadeus lived?
A *moat*-zart!

What did Frida say as she danced under the limbo stick?
"*Kah-lo* can you go?"

Why did Leonardo da Vinci buy a new pair of sneakers? For the *Run-aissance*.

What do you say to Frank Lloyd Wright when he sneezes? *"Guggenheim!"*

Knock! Knock!
Who's there?
Ear.
Ear who?
Ear you are, Mr. Mozart!

What does <u>Richard Branson</u> like to eat for breakfast?

Raisin *Bran-son*.

Why did Picasso take a deep breath on his birthday?
To *Pa-blow* out his candles!

Knock! Knock!
Who's there?
Steven.
Steven who?
Steven I know Spielberg is a great filmmaker!

DIRECTOR

Which one of Leonardo da Vinci's paintings complains a lot?
The *Moan-a Lisa*!

Why did **Richard Branson** try to fly around the world in a balloon?

To prove he wasn't full of *hot air*!

Which famous cartoonist got sick a lot? *Up-Chuck* Jones!

Knock! Knock!
Who's there?
Tinker Bell!
Tinker Bell who?
I *Tink-er-Bell* isn't **working,** Mr. Disney!

Why didn't **Walt Disney** use tile for the floors in Disneyland?

Because he preferred *Walt*-to-*Walt* carpeting!

**Knock!
Knock!**
Who's there?
Lucas.
Lucas who?
Luc-as though nothing is wrong and those Stormtroopers will leave you alone!

What did **Pablo Picasso's** mom say when he had a booger?

"Don't *Picasso* your nose!"

What does Walt Disney cook with?
A *Peter Pan*!

Knock! Knock!
Who's there?
Claude.
Claude who?
Claude my way up the hill to meet Monet!

Why did Andy Warhol buy a balloon?
Because he was making *pop* art!

**Knock!
Knock!**
Who's there?
Cindy Lou.
Cindy Lou who?
That's a character
Chuck Jones **knew!**

Why was Claude Monet so popular?
He always made a good first *impressionist*!

Why did →
George Lucas
go to the doctor?
He had Star *Warts*!

Why did <u>Bruce Lee</u> always practice martial arts?
He couldn't *kick* the habit.

Knock! Knock!

Who's there?

Apple.

Apple who?

A-pple **this rope and then** Houdini **magically appears!**

Who does Walt Disney call when he wants to play patty-cake?

Slapping Beauty!

Which of the Three Stooges took care of the yard work?

Moe.

Where does <u>Chuck Jones</u> go when he has a cold?

To see Dr. Seuss.

What did Houdini say when he got tired of riding the bus?

"Abra-*car*-dabra!"

Knock! Knock!
Who's there?
Silent.
Silent who?
Si-lent my cane to <u>Charlie Chaplin,</u> but he never gave it back!

Knock! Knock!

Who's there?

Cameron.

Cameron who?

Camera-n **film are two things** Steven Spielberg **uses a lot!**

Why was Annie Oakley afraid to move to the big city?

Because it was so *farm* away from home!

What magic trick did <u>Harry Houdini</u> do just by walking down the street?

He *turned* into a grocery store!

How come Annie Oakley
never ran out of bullets?
Because she used a *ri-full*!

**Knock!
Knock!**
Who's there?
Sadie.
Sadie who?
Sa-die **magic word and**
Houdini **will appear!**

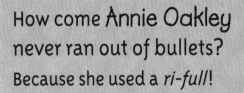

Why did
Maria Tallchief's
stomach hurt?
She had a *ballet*-ache!

120

Knock! Knock!
Who's there?
Bill.
Bill who?
Bill-dings designed by
Frank Lloyd Wright
are amazing!

What does Chuck Jones drive to work?
A *car*-toon!

What did
Annie Oakley
say when she
missed a target?
"Oh, shoot!"

What type of lumber did <u>Charlie Chaplin</u> use to build his house?

Holly-wood.

Knock!
Knock!
Who's there?
Noah.
Noah who?
No-ah **good place to see some** Claude Monet **paintings?**

What is Bruce Lee's favorite food?
Karate *chops*!

Knock!
Knock!
Who's there?
Imma.
Imma who?
Imm-a **big fan of** Lucille Ball!